If a FrOg Had a Santa

Nelle Whelchel Brannen
Author

Cathy Brownlee Wood
Illustrator

Archway Publishing books may be ordered through booksellers or by contacting:

Archway Publishing
1663 Liberty Drive
Bloomington, IN 47403
www.archwaypublishing.com
1 (888) 242-5904

ISBN: 978-1-4808-2677-9 (sc)
ISBN: 978-1-4808-2678-6 (e)

Print information available on the last page.

Archway Publishing rev. date: 02/29/2016

Dedicated

to the Glory of God.

"Love never fails."

1 Corinthians 13:8a (NIV)

Let Grandmother
tell you a story
That's as different as
different can be.
It's about some new
Santa Clauses:
Just turn the page
and you'll see.

I was rocking and just thinking
What joy there would be
If all creatures had Santas
Like you and like me.

If a frog had a Santa
He'd bring lily pads and flies.

A bird would be happy
With blue, sunny skies.

A mole would like holes
To play "peek-a-boo" in.

Fireflies would like weeds
To play "hide-and-blink" in.

A butterfly would flutter
To have pretty flowers.

A squirrel would want nuts
To hide by the hours.

Silver shoes for the horse
Would be just the thing.

While a cat would "meow"
For a ball of red string.

Dogs want bones
To bury and keep.

Hamsters want wheels
To spin with their feet.

**A duck would waddle
For a few grains of corn.**

The penguins want some ice
To slip and slide on.

A zebra wants some
stripes changed
Just for the season.

The owl "hoots" for a book:
That stands to reason.

A pig would like some mud
Just for the play.

An elephant wants peanuts and
Will give thanks with a sway.

Juicy worms for the fish

Make a special treat.

A hive for the bees
Would really be neat.

A camel needs
an umbrella
To keep out
of the sun.

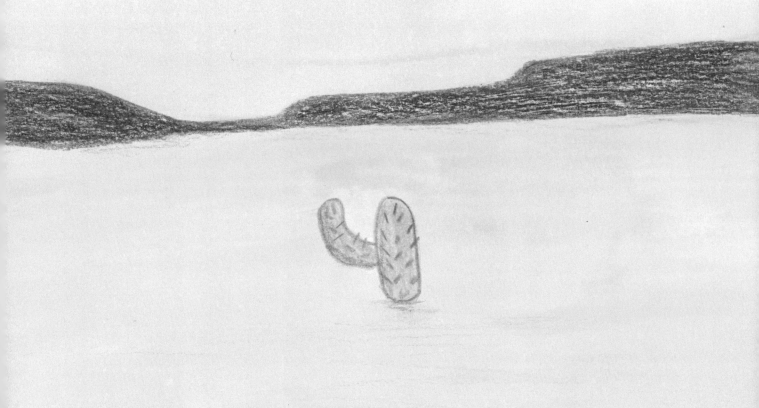

Kangaroos want boxing gloves
For some jabbing fun.

The lion would roar
For a jeweled crown.

Soft shoes for the mouse
So she won't make a sound.

It has taken lots of thought
To make this list.
Would you please take the time
And name creatures
I've missed?

My story ends here

but remember

one thing...

Love

is the GREATEST gift
any Santa can bring.

About the Author

Nelle Whelchel Brannen, author, was born in Anniston, Alabama on Easter Sunday, April 20, 1924, daughter of Myrtice Davis Whelchel and John Bruce Whelchel. She had one sister, Mary Jo Whelchel Kennedy.

She graduated from Anniston High School and received her college education from Shorter College, Rome, Georgia.

Nelle Whelchel and William Thomas Brannen married in Corpus Christi, Texas on August 21, 1943. He received his US Navy "Wings of Gold" the same day as their wedding. Their marriage has been enduring. They celebrated their 72nd anniversary on August 21, 2015. The couple had four children: Rebecca Brannen Wood (her husband is Henry Wood); William Thomas Brannen, Jr. (his wife is Maribeth); Alice Kay Brannen Collins (her husband is B. John Collins, Jr.); and David Randall Brannen (his wife is Claire). Grandchildren are William Keith Wood, Christopher Brannen Wood, William Braden Brannen (who passed away August 31, 2014), Courtney Collins Cawley (her husband is Chris), Kyle Collins Hitchcock (her husband is Andrew), Katherine Penn Brannen, Jane Elizabeth Brannen and John "Jack" Taylor Brannen. She rejoices also in her (to date) thirteen great grandchildren and remembers that "one of them is in heaven today."

After Mrs. Brannen's children all became school age, she sought employment outside the home. She worked for several years as a secretary in federal government agencies in the Atlanta area and throughout the United States. She retired in 1990.

She and her husband were active members of First Baptist Church, Marietta, Georgia. She was a member of the Cobb-Marietta Junior League where she worked actively for years. One of her favorite areas of volunteer service was with handicapped children in Creswell School. Now in retirement she is an Emeritus Sustainer of the Cobb-Marietta Junior League.

She and her husband volunteered to deliver Meals-on-Wheels. They made their home in Eatonton, GA after retirement, living there for 23 years. They are members of First United Methodist Church, Milledgeville.

In reviewing her life, Mrs. Brannen states: "I am a wife, mother, homemaker, grandmother, great grandmother. I was a secretary by profession for federal government agencies. I am a most blessed follower of the Lord Jesus Christ."

Mrs. Brannen is now a resident of Green Acres Nursing Home and her husband is a resident of Georgia War Veterans Home, both in Milledgeville. She is happy to have this book which she wrote for her grandchildren years ago published in the ninety-first year of her life.

About the Illustrator

(Photograph by Kyle Hitchcock Photography)

Cathy Brownlee Wood, illustrator, grew up in the Atlanta area where she attended the Arlington School first through twelfth grades. Long interested in art, Mrs. Wood received the Bachelor of Arts in Fine Arts as well as the Master of Education in Early Childhood Education at Georgia College and State University, Milledgeville.

Teaching has been her major work, with thirty-five years in the classroom. Her area of teaching has mainly been art. She is currently teaching art at the John Milledge Academy. She is especially drawn to children's art, as the illustrations in Mrs. Brannen's book indicate.

Mrs. Wood makes her home in Eatonton, Georgia with her husband Chris. Their two children, Cody and Casey, are in college. Her hobby is working with stained glass and making windows and other pieces of decorative art.

Mrs. Wood worked closely with Mrs. Nelle Brannen in producing the illustrations for _If a Frog Had a Santa_. The author wanted the book to bring delight and the imaginary animal characters to seem loving and happy. The artist sought to convey this spirit of love with her drawings.

Acknowledgement: Thanks to **Ethelene Dyer Jones**, Milledgeville, who gave editorial assistance to the author in the publication of this children's book. She has been a writer for many years and has assisted with editing eight books to date. In her professional life, she was a classroom teacher of English in both high school and college and was a school librarian. She was faculty advisor for her high school's student literary journal for 14 years, and spent over 30 years as an educator. Since retirement, she has been writing newspaper columns for 25 years. Poetry, devotional literature and history are also among her writing interests.

Printed in the United States
By Bookmasters